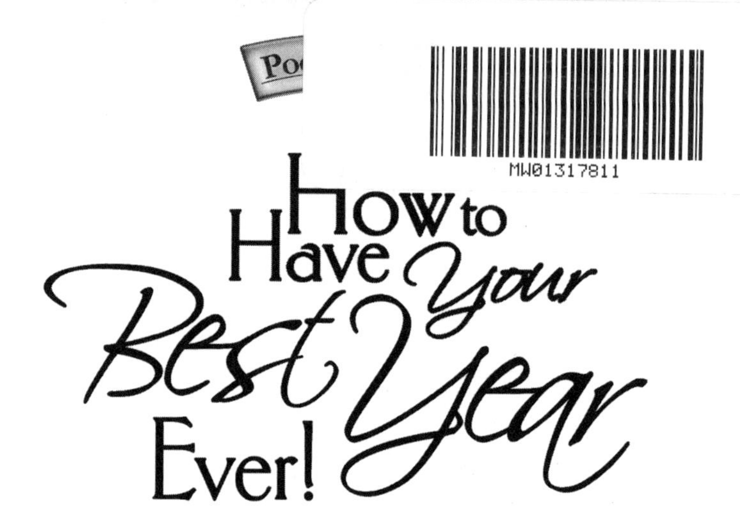

HONOR HB BOOKS

Inspiration and Motivation for the Seasons of Life

COOK COMMUNICATIONS MINISTRIES
Colorado Springs, Colorado • Paris, Ontario
KINGSWAY COMMUNICATIONS LTD
Eastbourne, England

Honor ® is an imprint of
Cook Communications Ministires, Colorado Springs, CO 80918
Cook Communications, Paris, Ontario
Kingsway Communications, Eastbourne, England

POCKET PLAN: HOW TO HAVE YOUR BEST YEAR EVER

Compiled by Shanna D. Gregor

Cover and Interior Design: BMB Design

First Printing, 2006
Printed in the United States of America

1 2 3 4 5 6 7 8 9 10 Printing/Year 11 10 09 08 07 06

ISBN 1-56292-750-7

Introduction

Each year people all over the world celebrate New Year's Eve with an attitude of "out with the old, in with the new" as the stroke of midnight turns our focus toward a brand new year. Many cheer with a heart full of dreams for a fresh start and the opportunity to make this the best year ever.

You now hold in your hand the *Pocket Plan: How to Have Your Best Year Ever.* It's filled with practical insight to help you make this year the best year you've ever had. You'll discover powerful wisdom, knowledgeable quotes, inspirational scriptures, witty ideas, and self-help checklists that give you the courage to make each day a successful part of your best year ever.

More people prove successful

by resolving to begin a new habit,

rather than striving to break an old one.

Cheers to a new year and another chance for us to get it right.

Oprah Winfrey

7 Keys to Successfully Achieve New Year's Resolutions:

1. SET REAL goals that you believe to be attainable.
2. IMAGINE how you will deal with the temptation and then see yourself performing that task successfully each time temptation crosses your mind.
3. MOTIVATE yourself by keeping a list of benefits your success will bring you.
4. TALK IT UP by sharing your resolution with friends and family who can offer you support.
5. REWARD yourself incrementally.
6. KEEP records of your success.
7. FORGIVE yourself if you slip up and start again by giving yourself a clean slate.

Have Your Best Year Ever . . .

Through Friendships

The glory of friendship is not the outstretched hand, nor the kindly smile, nor the joy of companionship;
it is the spiritual inspiration that comes to one when you discover that someone
else believes in you and is willing to trust you with a friendship.

Ralph Waldo Emerson

Friendship arises out of mere Companionship when two or more of the companions discover that they have in common some insight or interest or even taste which the others do not share and which, till that moment, each believed to be his own unique treasure (or burden). The typical expression of opening Friendship would be something like, "What? You too? I thought I was the only one." . . . It is when two such persons discover one another, when, whether with immense difficulties and semi-articulate fumblings or with what would seem to us amazing and elliptical speed, they share their vision—it is then that Friendship is born. And instantly they stand together in an immense solitude.

C. S. Lewis

Lasting Friendship

True friendship is often difficult to find and even more challenging to keep. It is dynamic and alive—something that we need to cultivate and nurture. Friendships change and hopefully grow as we cultivate them with positive, loving behavior.

Most friendships don't happen instantly but as we open up and become vulnerable to each other, we are allowed deeper access into the other's world. As we are honest with each other to be who God created us to be, we can develop a strong foundation of friendships. Sharing your sorrows and joys, taking the good with the bad, forgiving and being forgiving brings richness to relationship. Being a good friend is what truly produces good friends in your life.

Relationships begin with a greeting, then a drawing to discover more about one another, and as you learn about the other, then you decide if there is a connection—a bond of a lasting friendship.

Seeds That Encourage Friendship:

- A smile
- Saying "thank you"
- Words of appreciation
- Words of affirmation
- Compliments
- A listening ear
- Compassion
- A shoulder to cry on
- Willingness to cheer others on

Seasons of Friendship

Friends come and go for all kinds of reasons: moving, busyness, divorce, illness, or personal transition. Sometimes friends "grow apart" and meet other friends, develop new interests, or withdraw in a time of difficulty or change. Any of these things can weaken or even end a friendship.

Sometimes God allows the paths of our lives and hearts to cross for a season. If this happens, don't fret and don't regret. Be thankful that you were able to share part of your life with someone you really enjoyed.

Realize too, that some friendships develop quickly and others take more time. Remain open to the pace that God allows.

Perhaps you become very close to a next door neighbor and share an exciting season of raising your children together, but times change and you move away from that special person. Recognize that relationship is a gift from God, even if only given for a season. But when you risk a chance to know someone you may be very fortunate to gain a gift of friendship that can last a lifetime.

When we're willing to invest in one another we discover more about ourselves.

The season when to come and when to go, to sing or cease to sing, we never know.
Alexander Pope

A winter in friendship can blossom into a glorious spring.

I Promise

One way to dampen the sparks of friendship is to let someone down by not keeping your word. Don't say yes to a friend and then backpedal or forget to honor your commitment. Adults can be just as disappointed as children when something they were looking forward to doesn't happen, especially when it's due to an oversight.

Keep a calendar if you have a tendency to double book or overbook yourself. Keep a wall calendar at home and a small calendar that you can carry with you when you leave the house. Make a point to update (or at least look at) your calendar each day.

Great friends keep their commitments.

A promise is a terrible thing to break!

And I can live my life on earth
Contented to the end,
If but a few shall know my worth
And proudly call me friend.
Edgar A. Guest

As iron sharpens iron, so a man sharpens the countenance of his friend.
Proverbs 27:17 NKJV

Treasure Hunt

A true friend is one who knows all your faults, never gives up, and loves you anyway. We all long for a friend like that, a person with whom we can share our secret dreams, fears, and insecurities—a person who will never abandon us, even if we mess up, lose everything, or become a permanent burden. Of course, if that's what we're all looking for, then we have the whole process backward. Far more important than finding a true friend is being a true friend. We need to be that friend we're looking for. We need to be the one who never gives up, even when we've been hurt, misunderstood, or rejected. We should also be willing to confront and correct with love.

Take a good look at the kind of friend you are, and develop an openness in your relationships that removes all fear of abandonment or discovery. Be the first to accept and love unconditionally in your relationships.

Friendship is often the glue that keeps us from falling apart.

He who finds a faithful friend finds a treasure.

If one falls down, his friend can help him up. But pity the man who falls and has no one to help him up!
Ecclesiastes 4:10 NIV

Today a man discovered gold and fame,

Another higher flew the stormy seas;

Another set an unarmed world aflame,

One found the germ of disease.

But what high fates my path attend:

For I—today I found a friend.

Samuel Johnson

A mirror reflects a man's face, but what he is really like is shown by the kind of friends he chooses.

Proverbs 27:19 TLB

The best mirror is an old friend.

George Herbert

There is in all of us a sense of incompleteness that can only be eased when we are in relationship with other people.

Rich Hurst

Friends

- Refuse to allow friends to face difficulty alone
- Keep confidences
- Believe the very best of others
- Offer compliments and encouragement
- Let their guard down
- Are prompt
- Offer wise counsel
- Offer hospitality without grumbling
- Look to invest in the lives of others
- Actively listen
- Show up and show support
- Stand ready to celebrate

A Ready Reception

Hospitality is a concept that seems old-fashioned in our fast-paced, self-oriented world. Webster's defines it as "generous and cordial reception; ready reception." After a long, hard day at the office, being hospitable sounds like a tall order, doesn't it? Just the same, laying out the welcome mat can be an incredible gift to someone who is lonely or new in the community. It's a kind gesture for the friends you already have. Being hospitable will serve to solidify current friendships and help you initiate new ones. And most people won't care if you live in a grand mansion or a tiny apartment. They just know it feels good to be welcomed into your home and into your life. There are friends waiting just outside your door.

Offer hospitality to one another without grumbling.
1 Peter 4:9 NIV

Friends are helpful not only because they will listen to us, but because they will laugh at us; Through them we learn a little objectivity, a little modesty, a little courtesy; We learn the rules of life and become better players of the game.
Will Durant

When a friend is in trouble, don't annoy him by asking if there is anything you can do. Think up something appropriate and do it.

Sir Phillip Sydney

Having and being a friend means wanting only the best for each other.

Alexandra Stoddard

You can make more friends in two months by becoming more interested in other people than you can in two years by trying to get people interested in you.

Honor one another above yourselves.

Romans 12:10 NIV

When I talk to my closest female friends, I feel my soul being sunned and watered when they ask questions, drawing out the deep waters of my soul, and when they empathize, rejoicing when I rejoice, weeping when I weep. I can't count the number of times my heart has been gladdened by women: an affirming e-mail, a heartfelt hug, a gift of my favorite hazelnut skinny latte from Starbucks, or a green and thriving plant growing as our friendship grows.

Dee Brestin

"Stay" is a charming word in a friend's vocabulary.
Amos Bronson Alscott

Something like home that is not home is to be desired; it is found in the house of a friend.
Sir William Temple

Have Your Best Year Ever...

With Your Family

The only rock I know that stays steady, the only institution I know that works is the family.

Lee Iacocca

There's a special kind of closeness
That only families know,
That begins with childhood trust
And deepens as you grow,
There's a special kind of happiness
In sharing little things,
The laughter, smiles, & quiet talks
That daily living brings.
There's a special kind of comfort
In knowing your family's there
To back you up, to cheer you up,
To understand & care.
Of all the treasures life may bring
Your family means the most.
And whether near or far apart
That love will hold you close.

Anonymous

The family is both the fundamental unit of society as well as the root of culture. It represents a child's initial source of unconditional love and acceptance and provides lifelong connectedness with others. The family is the first setting in which socialization takes place and where children learn to live with mutual respect for one another. A family is where a child learns to display affection, control his temper, and pick up his toys. Finally, a family is a perpetual source of encouragement, advocacy, assurance, and emotional refueling that empowers a child to venture with confidence into the greater world and to become all that he can be.

Marianne E. Neifert

The lack of emotional security of our American young people is due, I believe, to their isolation from the larger family unit. No two people—no mere father and mother—as I have often said, are enough to provide emotional security for a child. He needs to feel himself one in a world of kinfolk, persons of variety in age and temperament, and yet allied to himself by an indissoluble bond which he cannot break if he could, for nature has welded him into it before he was born.

Pearl S. Buck

7 Actions That Produce Successful Families:

1. Make your family your highest priority.
2. Encourage honest expression of thoughts and feelings for effective communication.
3. Fairly distribute responsibility according to age among the siblings.
4. Take time for yourself so you can be your very best for your family.
5. Offer stability through family traditions, relationships, and routines.
6. Accentuate the positive—especially in front of your children.
7. Celebrate your successes individually and as a family.

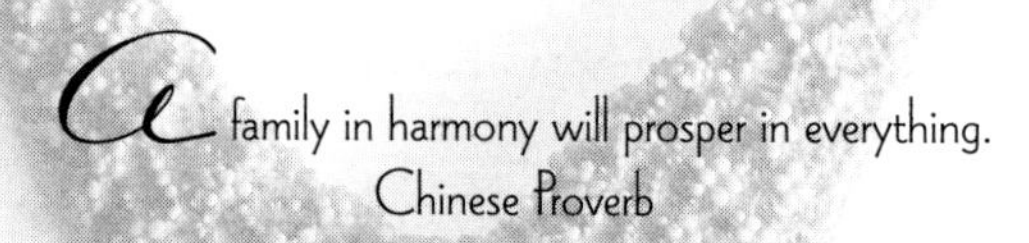

A family in harmony will prosper in everything.

Chinese Proverb

A life-long blessing for children is to fill them with warm memories of times together. Happy memories become treasures in the heart to pull out on the tough days of adulthood.

Charlotte Davis Kasl

Loving relationships are a family's best protection against the challenges of the world.

Bernie Wiebe

To maintain a joyful family requires much from both the parents and the children. Each member of the family has to become, in a special way, the servant of the others.

Pope John Paul II

Time—Children Want Lots of It!

We hear it all the time—parents must spend time with their children. Younger children obviously need more attention, but to think our preteens and teenagers can fend for themselves is a mistake. Sure, they may act as if they don't need us, but they do—whether they realize it or not.

Making a living, serving in a volunteer capacity, maintaining a household—all of these things drain the time we should be giving our children. Often we feel little control over those things that crowd our schedules, but if we've lost control to that extent, the problem lies with us, not with the schedule.

We need to look carefully at how we spend our time. What activities can be eliminated? How can we include our children in some of the time-consuming tasks for which we're responsible? It's never too late to make changes that may secure a child's future.

You'll never regret placing your children above your other commitments in life.

Children are not casual guests in our home. They have been loaned to us temporarily for the purpose of loving them and instilling a foundation of values on which their future lives will be built.
James Dobson

No success can compensate for missing the mark in preparing your child for his future.

Cheer Them On

Part of our role as family members is to be a "fan" of those with whom we live. WE are to be the number one cheerleader for our spouse and children. In return we receive the knowledge that they are hoping we will succeed in every area of our own life.

E-N-C-O-U-R-A-G-E-M-E-N-T is perhaps the best cheer you can learn!

E is for Enthusiasm and Energy in supporting causes important to your family members.

N is for saying "Next time you'll succeed."

C is for Compassion.

O is for Open lines of communication.

U is for Understanding.

R is for Rooting on the team.

A is for Arranging your schedule to make time for others in your family.

G is for Going the extra mile.

E is for Entertaining your children's friends.

M is for Modeling a positive attitude.

E is for Empowering your child with wisdom.

N is for Never giving up.

T is for Taking time out for hugs and praise.

We should seize every opportunity to give encouragement. Encouragement is oxygen for the soul.
Ruth Graham Bell

Encourage one another daily, as long as it is called Today.
Hebrews 3:13 NIV

The Power of Touch

Touch is powerful. Make sure you use it wisely to accentuate the positive and never to demonstrate anger or frustration.

A tap on the shoulder. A kiss to the forehead. The brush of your hand. A warm embrace. Your family members consider them all to be signs of affection that say, without a word, I love you. They find support through your touch that says, I'm here for you. I understand.

No matter what their day brings, you can offer them assurance. With each touch you build them up and offer strength. You give your spouse confidence to make it through the day. You show your children you believe in them without words.

Do not boast about tomorrow, for you do not know what a day may bring forth.

Proverbs 27:1 NIV

Your life consists of moments. Don't waste a single one.

Single moments are where real life takes place.

How beautiful is youth! How bright it gleams with its illusions, aspirations, dreams!
Henry Wadsworth Longfellow

Lighten Up

Sometimes we just need to loosen up, lighten up, and think with the heart of a child. In the movie *Young Frankenstein*, Dr. Frankenstein is saying good-bye to his sweetheart, Elizabeth. He steps to embrace her but is immediately rebuffed with, "The hair. The hair." All his attempts to bid her an affectionate adieu are foiled because she doesn't want anything "mussed."

That's exactly how some people live their lives. As adults, many of us need the childlike enthusiasm that will allow us to loosen up and live.

You can't make a positive difference in the lives of others by becoming a dreary old fuddy-dud. Engage in some of the activities and thought processes that made childhood unique. Lie on the ground and watch the clouds roll by, do a cannonball off the diving board, play a game of hide-and-seek with a three-year-old, throw your arms around your family and hug them without reserve. These activities are sure to give you a new lease on life and brighten the world of those around you.

A torn jacket is soon mended, but hard words bruise the heart of a child.
Henry Wadsworth Longfellow

An Apology

"I'm sorry" isn't an easy phrase to say, but it can work miracles. It's the first step to resolving differences and restoring relationships in your home. It relieves the stress of hard feelings or silence. Admitting you were insensitive, short-tempered, or just plain wrong is a hard lesson in humility especially when it involves your spouse or children.

It may not change how someone feels immediately, but it demonstrates that you are willing to take responsibility for your actions—a message your family, especially your children, need to hear.

Asking for forgiveness goes a step further. It expresses more than just admitting your guilt. It voices the desire for reconciliation and esteems your family as valuable. Your children realize they are important enough to you to invest in them and put forth the effort to get it right.

Never, never be too proud to say, "I'm sorry" to your child when you've made a mistake.

Humility, like darkness, reveals the heavenly lights.
Henry David Thoreau

Show your children the same respect that you expect from them.

Sometimes the greatest treasures you'll ever discover are hidden in the heart of your child.

Have Your Best Year Ever . . .

In Your Marriage

All married couples should learn the art of battle as they should learn the art of making love. Good battle is objective and honest—never vicious or cruel. Good battle is healthy and constructive, and brings to a marriage the principle of equal partnership.

Ann Landers

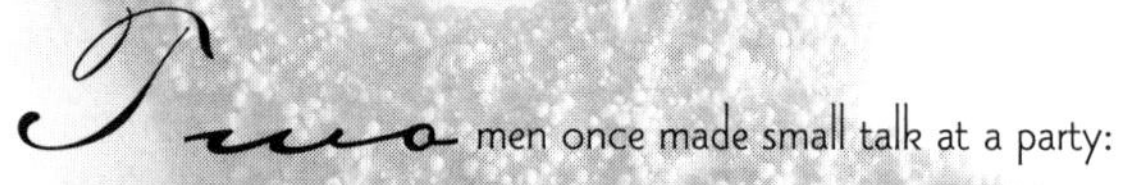 men once made small talk at a party:

"You and your wife seem to get along very well," one man said. "Don't you ever have differences?"

"Sure," said the other. "We often have differences, but we get over them quickly."

"How do you do that?" the first man asked.

"Simple," said the second, "I don't tell her we have them."

The kind of music people should have in their homes is domestic harmony.

Choosing a Positive Focus

We tend to choose either a negative or positive path for our marriage by the thoughts, feelings, and perceptions we have as we build our marriage. You may be starting your journey or enjoying your twenty-fifth wedding anniversary, but the life you live tomorrow is influenced by the way you think today.

The direction of your thought life can determine the course of your marriage. You can choose to emphasize and concentrate on what your spouse does wrong, what you don't like, or want to change; or you can set your eyes on what drew you to them in the first place. Remember the little things that singled them out to be the one for you.

Your eyes are in front of you so that you can go where you're looking. The same is true in your marriage. If you focus on your spouse's shortcomings, they'll always be the most prominent thing you'll see in your wedding picture.

However, if your daily quest is to find and affirm the positive qualities in your spouse, you'll find a newness to your relationship. If you have trouble, start small and make notes that remind you:

He left the toilet seat down just for me.

She remembered to squeeze the toothpaste from the bottom of the tube.

He bought the flavor of coffee that I prefer instead of his kind.

No matter what your age or length of marriage, you can start now, adding to your marriage to make it even more fulfilling. Practice a positive focus.

Blessings for a Marriage

By James D. Freeman

May your marriage bring you all the exquisite excitements a marriage should bring, and may life grant you also patience, tolerance, and understanding.

May you always need one another—not so much to fill your emptiness as to help you to know your fullness. A mountain needs a valley to be complete; the valley does not make the mountain less, but more; and the valley is more a valley because it has a mountain towering over it. So let it be with each of you.

May you need one another but not out of weakness. May you want one another, but not out of lack. May you entice one another, but not compel one another. May you embrace one another, but not encircle one another.

May you succeed in all important ways with one another, but not fail in the little graces. May you look for things to praise, often say, "I love you!" and take no notice of small faults. If you have quarrels that push you apart, may both of you hope to have good sense enough to take the first step back.

May you enter into the mystery which is the awareness of one another's presence—no more physical than spiritual, warm and near when you are side by side, and warm and near when you are in separate rooms or even distant cities. May you have happiness, and may you find it making one another happy.

May you have love and may you find it loving one another!

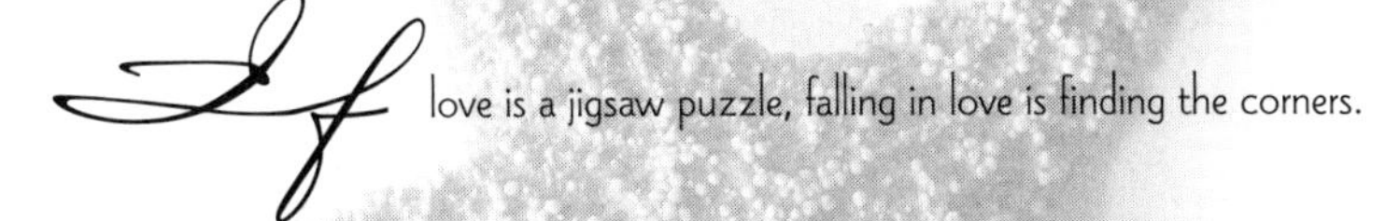

If love is a jigsaw puzzle, falling in love is finding the corners.

What a happy and holy fashion it is that those who love one another should rest on the same pillow.
Nathaniel Hawthorne

I married the first man I ever kissed. When I tell this to my children, they just about throw up.
Barbara Bush

My most brilliant achievement was my ability to be able to persuade my wife to marry me.
Winston Churchill

Say It

The paper was poorly folded. The writing was smudged and crooked. The verse didn't rhyme, and the cutout of the heart made less than a perfect Valentine. But the message from her husband, who'd recently suffered a stroke and had difficulty with his motor skills was very clear: "I love you."

Don't wait to express your love to your spouse. No matter how you package it, this gift is certain to bring an excitement to your relationship. Not doing so can only bring you a heart full of regret when the opportunity is lost. It takes so little in the way of time, energy, and resources. Such a simple act is as much for yourself as it is for them. The most important words in the English language are "I love you!"

Speech both conceals and reveals the thoughts of men.
Dionysius Cato

Measure with Love

During the course of their twenty-four years of marriage, Tom accumulated a fortune in the natural gas business. But then in a twenty-four month period, he saw the fruit of his labors slip away to creditors and foreclosures. Things became so desperate at one point that in order to make the monthly payment on their house, he had to sell his wife's engagement ring. Finally Tom was forced out of the oil business altogether. He and Tina lost everything they had.

When things looked the worst, Tom landed a promising job in another industry and slowly began to come out of his personal and professional slump. Nearly two years later while out to dinner, Tina saw in her husband signs of his old exuberance.

When Tom took his wife's hand in his own and said, "Tina, you are like this diamond—beautiful, exquisite, precious," she thought her heart would burst.

"But where did you get the money?" she asked as he put the ring on her finger.

"You haven't known it," Tom confessed, "but for two years I've been giving plasma once a week. I saved all the money I was paid, and last week I sold my hunting gear. The only hunting I want to do from now on is hunt for ways to love you more. You are my life."

The measure of a man is not how great his faith is, but how great his love is.

7 Rules for a Good Clean Fight:

Author Charlie W. Shedd shares "Our Seven Official Rules for a Good, Clean Fight" in a book he wrote to his daughter, *Letters to Karen*:

1. Before we begin we must both agree that the time is right.
2. We will remember that our only aim is to deepen understanding.
3. We will check our weapons often to be sure they're not deadly.
4. We will lower our voices one notch instead of raising them two.
5. We will never quarrel or reveal private matters in public.
6. We will discuss an armistice whenever either of us calls "halt."
7. When we have come to terms, we will put it away till we both agree it needs more discussing.

Says Shedd, "No small part of the zest in a good marriage comes from working through differences. Learning to zig and zag with the entanglements; studying each other's reactions under pressure; handling one another's emotions intelligently—all these offer a challenge that simply can't be beat for sheer fun and excitement."

An argument is the longest distance between two points.

When angry, do not sin; do not ever let your wrath
(your exasperation, your fury or indignation) last until the sun goes down.

Ephesians 4:26 AB

The difference between smooth sailing and shipwreck in marriage lies in what you as a couple are doing about the rough weather.

Matrimony—the high sea for which no compass has been invented.
Heine

There are three things too wonderful for me to understand—no, four!
. . . How a ship finds its way across the heaving ocean.
The growth of love between a man and a [woman]
Proverbs 30:18-19 TLB

You have a lifetime to enjoy one another. Don't waste a day of it.

Think Twice

We're never satisfied with what we have. We fall in love with a person who has so many qualities that we admire—qualities we wish we could lay claim to. Then within a few years, we wish that same person, now our spouse, would think more like we do. In time, the word "incompatible" starts to creep into our thoughts about our marriage.

Most differences between a husband and wife, though, represent strength, not weakness. Once we come to terms with this, we can stop trying to think alike and start putting our heads together to come up with creative solutions to problems in our relationship and in our life together.

Don't expect your spouse to be like you. Instead, cherish the individual distinctions that, when combined, create a whole new creation in marriage. When you allow this new creation to flourish, you strengthen your marriage and find unity.

Marriage has in it less of beauty, but more of safety, than the single life. It has more care, but less danger; it is more merry, and more sad. It is fuller of sorrows, and fuller of joys; it lies under more burdens, but it is supported by all the strengths of love and charity, and those burdens are delightful.

Ronald Reagan

A young woman once phoned her mother and cried, "Mother, I had no idea marriage meant washing and ironing so many shirts!"

Her mother wisely counseled, "Think of each shirt you iron as an act of love."

The young woman took her mother's advice and just below the neckline on each collar she ironed, she planted a big kiss, one complete with a tint of lipstick.

10 Questions to Ask Yourself about Your Ability to Give and Take

Are you willing:

1. to give silence when your spouse needs a little quiet time?
2. to take a rebuke and let it rest unchallenged?
3. to give your spouse the benefit of the doubt?
4. to take on the extra chores when your spouse is stressed out?
5. to give a word of spontaneous encouragement?
6. to take time to spend with your spouse—alone and without interruption?
7. to give your spouse the courtesy of "please" and "thank you."
8. to take a time out when a disagreement seems to be overheating?
9. to give a compliment?
10. to take criticism?

Be gentle and ready to forgive; never hold grudges.

Colossians 3:13 TLB

Have Your Best Year Ever . . .

In Your Finances

The man who will use his skill and constructive imagination to see how much he can give for a dollar, instead of how little he can give for a dollar, is bound to succeed.

Henry Ford

The American consumer is facing dire financial straits. . . . Our nation's financial situation, with record budget deficits and bank failures, is deplorable. However, the nation's situation is only a reflection of our own personal inability to "just say no" to ourselves. Our failure to get control of financial matters in our personal lives will have to be rectified before we can demand accountability from elected officials. . . . the good of the family is often overlooked so Dad or Mom can have that special trinket they must possess.

Dave Ramsey

Money Matters

People spend more time thinking about money and family finances than probably any other topic. It has been a point of contention in the home for decades. Whether you have plenty or not enough—you very likely spend a lot of brainpower contemplating how to get it, or how to spend it.

Men want to be successful in providing for their family while women desire a sense of security. Finding common ground no matter which part of the financial levee you're standing on brings great debate to the dinner table.

Financial planners tell you to save, budget, and invest. Your charities ask you to give. Your children want the latest, greatest shoes, clothes, and technical gadgets. The wheel of fortune spins so hard and fast that sometimes you're surprised to still be standing when you finally get off.

Billy Graham said, "If a person gets his attitude toward money straight, it will help straighten out almost every other area of his life." We must take control of our finances and become determined to make money serve us, instead of being the servants of money.

We make a living by what we get—we make a life by what we give.
Winston Churchill

If money is your hope for independence you will never have it. The only real security that a man will have in this world is a reserve of knowledge, experience, and ability.
Henry Ford

Wealth to us is not mere material for vainglory but an opportunity for achievement.
Thucydides

The Race to Acquire

Stop trying to keep up with the Joneses. So often we are tempted to define our lives by what we own and how much we possess in comparison to other people. The standard may not be the Joneses—it may be the ideal of the "good life" or the examples of the affluence we see on television and in the movies.

The snare to "have it all" can result in entrapment to debt and the emotional bondage of low self-esteem. Balance and moderation slide away when greed sets in.

Choose instead to establish your self-worth on the basis of virtue and character. It is also important to make a distinction between wants and needs, and to be grateful for what is, rather than what isn't.

The race to acquire more is a never ending race. Don't sign up to compete.

The things that matter most should never be at the mercy of the things which matter least.
Johann Wolfgang Von Goethe

"Don't Get Rich Again"

The children of a very wealthy family were put into the care of a very qualified nanny, as well as a host of other servants the family employed. When adverse market trends impacted the family's finances, the family moved into a slightly smaller home, but they kept the children's nanny. Eventually, the family's financial situation became severe enough that they had to let the beloved nanny go.

One evening after the father returned home from a day of great anxiety and business worry, his little girl climbed up on his knee and threw her arms around his neck. "I love you, papa," she said, trying to soothe the weariness she intuitively perceived in him.

"I love you too, darling," the father replied, glad to have such a warm welcome home.

The little girl then said, "Papa, will you make me a promise?"

The father said, "What is it?"

So she said, "Papa, please promise me you won't get rich again. You never came to see us when you were rich, but now we can see you every night and hug you and kiss you and climb on your knee. Please don't get rich again!"

Children should know there are limits to family finances or they will confuse "we can't afford that" with "they don't want me to have it." The first statement is a realistic and objective assessment of a situation, while the other carries an emotional message.

Jean Ross Peterson

Jesus said, "Your heart will always be where your riches are."
Matthew 6:21 GNT

Christmas All Year Round

By the time Christmas rolls around each year, many of us find that we are too exhausted or too broke to enjoy the celebration. That's because we've spent two or three weeks before Christmas in the flurry of baking, cleaning, decorating, signing cards, and buying and wrapping gifts.

Who says you can't buy Christmas all year round? Try purchasing two or three gifts a month throughout the year. Wrap and label them so that you can remember what they are, and who they're for. Christmas cards can be signed and addressed well in advance also.

This approach makes life a little simpler and saves you money. Cards and gifts are less expensive in January than December.

The best Christmas gift we can give ourselves is time.

Commit to the LORD whatever you do, and your plans will succeed.
Proverbs 16:3 NIV

The real measure of our wealth is how much we'd be worth if we lost all of our money.

John Henry Jowett

Money and success don't change people; they merely amplify what is already there.

Will Smith

My idea of being rich—or at least of feeling rich—is to have no debts, mortgage, or overdraft and to be able to pay all bills by return post. This may seem a fairly modest ambition, but if everyone in the West were in this position our societies would indeed merit the term "affluent," and the world would be a much happier place.

Paul Johnson

Pay as You Go

Reader's Digest once printed an article from *Money* magazine entitled, "Win Your War Against Debt." In the middle of the article there was an advertisement for a popular anti-depressant. The irony of the placement of this ad may not have been intentional, but it conveyed a truth—debt can be depressing. Almost nothing zaps joy like a stack of unpaid bills marked "past due."

Some debt is unavoidable, but most indebtedness is self-inflicted. A "pay-as-you-go" policy is the best way to get out of debt and stay out of debt. And the happiness of a debt-free life cannot be calculated.

Happiness cannot be purchased.

Let no debt remain outstanding, except the continuing debt to love one another.
Romans 13:8 NIV

No More Debt

If you're in debt, get out now before you become so accustomed to it that it seems normal. Others may say, "Well, that's just the way it is. It's impossible to make ends meet without going into debt." Don't believe it. If you've come to rely on credit cards, or you can't imagine a time when you won't have at least one car to pay off, then it will be hard to change your way of thinking—no doubt about it. Paying down debt can be done!

Start by acknowledging the problem to yourself and to your spouse. Seek someone to help you. A reputable debt counseling service may be a good place to start. With a foundation of understanding freedom from debt, the lesson you learn can last a lifetime, long after you've eliminated the debt.

Freedom from debt returns the control of your finances to you.

7 Clues to Stretch the Family Budget

1. Establish a realistic budget. Make it flexible enough that your goals are attainable without adding so much pressure that you can't reach your goals.
2. Menu planning will cut back the cost. Plan family favorites around a certain dollar amount per meal, but include a small splurge once or twice a month as a special treat.
3. Cut personal debt and refuse to add dollars to your creditor's pocket.
4. Entertain at home. Discover low-cost or free activities you enjoy doing as a family (i.e. family game night, outdoor picnic).
5. Assess your definitions of "need" and "want."
6. Shop the services you must have by searching for companies that offer the same value at a lower cost.
7. Refinance whatever you can at a lower percentage rate or a quicker payoff.

Giving frees us from the familiar territory of our own needs by opening our mind to the unexplained worlds occupied by the needs of others.

Barbara Bush

Generosity lies less in giving much than in giving at the right moment.

Jean De La Bruyère

There is no beautifier of complexion, or form, or behavior, like the wish to scatter joy and not pain around us. 'Tis good to give a stranger a meal, or a night's lodging. 'Tis better to be hospitable to his good meaning and thought, and give courage to a companion. We must be as courteous to a man as we are to a picture, which we are willing to give the advantage of a good light.

Ralph Waldo Emerson

Anonymous Giving

We all like to be recognized for the nice things we do. Therefore many people never experience the deep satisfaction that comes with giving anonymously. As good as it feels to hear "thank you," it feels even better to know that your gift was given freely, without expectation.

Don't think of giving only in terms of money. You can enrich the lives of others in many ways—a freshly baked pie left on the doorstep, a note of encouragement in the mailbox—the variations are endless. If you've never given an anonymous gift, begin to look for opportunities. Then act! You will quickly find that you are making a difference in the lives of others as well as in your own life. Remember, no baggage accompanies an anonymous gift.

In God We Trust

To say that Emily's husband was tight with money would have been an understatement. A friend once said to him, "Kirk, you can squeeze a penny so hard it cries." Emily, on the other hand, enjoyed an occasional splurge or impulse purchase.

After they married, Kirk insisted that Emily account for every penny she spent and that she consult with him on any expenditure over $5. She went along with this dictum for a few months, but eventually felt such strict control was destroying her spontaneity and sense of fun in life. So she issued an ultimatum to Kirk: "Give me a household allowance, but don't question my use of a single penny of it."

At first Kirk was frightened to lose control. What if Emily overspent and he had to come up with even more than he had agreed upon? Emily reminded him that she had once managed her own money quite nicely. So Kirk agreed to give the new plan a 90-day trial.

At the end of the three-month period, Kirk not only admitted that he enjoyed the surprises that Emily brought into their life, but he increased the amount of money he allowed her to manage. And within two years, Kirk was giving himself an allowance and turning the rest of the budget over to Emily.

How calmly may we commit ourselves to the hands of him who bears up the world.
Jean Paul Richter

Have Your Best Year Ever . . .

In Your Health

For he who has health has hope; and he who has hope, has everything.
Owen Arthur

I have enjoyed greatly the second blooming that comes when you finish the life of the emotions and of personal relations; and suddenly find—at the age of fifty, let's say—that a whole new life has opened before you, filled with things you can think about, study, or read about.... It is as if a fresh sap of ideas and thoughts was rising in you.

Agatha Christie

In order to live life to the fullest, we need to be healthy in every area of life. Mental and emotional health is just as important as physical health. Your thoughts contribute to the stability of your mind, will, and emotions.

Learning to balance your world takes effort and courage in the middle of the ups and downs in life. Every person is unique and handles situations individually. The key to successfully navigating life is to understand yourself and how you respond to both the positive and negative ebbs and flows in the course of your life.

No man has the right to dictate what other men should perceive, create or produce, but all should be encouraged to reveal themselves, their perceptions and emotions, and to build confidence in the creative spirit.

Ansel Adams

If You Think You Can, You Can!

When do you concede failure? Is it when the ink is dry, the presentation has been made, or your friend has rejected you for the umpteenth time? What may look like failure could be an extended pause that allows you to see how strong, courageous, and firm you really are. Consider it a first failure instead of a final one. The ultimate failure can only come if you give up for good.

Think long and hard before you do that. Many a blockbuster best seller has been rejected dozens of times before finally seeing print. The sports world abounds with athletes who refused to pack it in, even after suffering humiliating defeats before tens of thousands of spectators. Stay the course and see it through. Where failure is tolerated, success finds its greatest opportunity.

It is the mind which creates the world about us, and even though we stand side by side in the same meadow, my eyes will never see what is beheld by yours, my heart will never stir to the emotions with which yours is touched.

George Gissing

I think that age as a number is not nearly as important as health. You can be in poor health and be pretty miserable at 40 or 50. If you're in good health, you can enjoy things into your 80s.

Bob Barker

Life is most delightful when it is on a downward slope.

Seneca

Age is a sacred trust.

A Record of Your Days

Getting older is a lot more than adding wrinkles, submitting to aches and pains, and watching your children leave home. Age is a record of your days. And it bears gifts—namely wisdom and confidence.

TO DO:

1. Continue to celebrate those birthdays.
2. Think back over the challenges you have conquered in the past year.
3. Remember the victories, and cherish new accomplishments.
4. Catalog the insights you've recently acquired.
5. Be thankful for every single day.

Laugh

Lighten up! There are few situations in life that can't be improved by a good, healthy sense of humor. We take things so seriously these days. People are all too easily offended. We're ready to sue at the drop of hat—or shake our fists in self-righteous anger at some injustice. We're thin-skinned, thickheaded, and not a lot of fun to be with.

Yes, there may be some serious problems in our world. All the more reason to keep it light when it comes to less important things. Can you remember a catastrophe in your past that you approached as if the world was coming to an end? The world just kept on spinning, though, and now you can probably chuckle at your reaction then. Look at your present circumstances in the same way—and realize that down the road, you look back in amusement.

Maintaining a sense of humor will help you weather the storms of life.

Our light affliction, which is but for a moment, worketh for us a far more exceeding and eternal weight of glory.

2 Corinthians 4:17 KJV

With the fearful strain that is on me night and day, if I did not laugh I should die.

Nathaniel Hawthorne

If I really wanted to beat stress I would:

- Stop playing the Lone Ranger and ask for help.
- Recognize that image isn't everything.
- Let go of the past.
- Refuse to live in the future.
- Cultivate quiet.
- Just say no.
- Pause and reflect.
- Live in the moment.
- Be more spontaneous.
- Limit my time with high-speed people.

Live Your Own Story

Watching television looks like a relaxing activity, and relaxation means stress-reducing, right? Not necessarily. Research has shown that people usually feel worse after spending time watching TV, not better. Television's main benefit is diversion, now and then, but when turning on the TV is as automatic as eating dinner every night, it can become a means of procrastination instead of relaxation. It replaces chores that need to be done, bills that need to be paid, and relationships that could use a little personal time.

Tonight, why not put down the remote and give your brain a workout with a good book. Or just sit back and watch the sunset. It's never a rerun.

Don't miss your own real life drama.

Take a Break

Life is tough for chronic overachievers. They chase after a "to do" list that would be impossible for any normal human being, consistently set themselves up for failure, and live under a dark cloud of guilt and fatigue. Even worse, they often project unrealistic expectations of those around them.

If you are an overachiever, for heaven's sake give yourself a break. It's possible to make a difference in the world without risking our physical and emotional health. Take a serious look at your obligations for the next month and weed out those that can be handled by someone else. Deal with your failures and put them behind you. Set aside time every day for rest and quiet contemplation. Reaching too far out can cause you to lose your grip.

How can we expect charity toward others, when we are uncharitable to ourselves?
Sir Thomas Browne

Relaxation

How long has it been since you took a vacation? Not a few days tacked onto a business trip? Not a whirlwind tour of twelve countries in six days. Not time off from work to catch up on projects around the house. A real vacation means relaxation.

Everyone needs a little downtime. Whether it's a long weekend or the luxury of a week or two, forsake deadlines. Read. Walk. Become deeply engrossed in conversations about life, love, faith—anything but work—with someone you care about.

If sitting in one place for too long drives you nuts, go for a bike ride, play tennis, swim. Just don't turn your vacation into another "got to do" list.

Take time to unwind from the daily grind.

He makes me lie down in green pastures, he leads me beside quiet waters, he restores my soul.
Psalm 23:2-3 NIV

A Little Appreciation

Many people spend their lives searching for happiness. In the end, some are fortunate enough to realize that it isn't about having, doing, or being more. It is about how we view what is already ours.

Look around you today and appreciate the riches God has placed in your life. Even if your circumstances are troubling and your prospects seem slim, you can always revel in the vibrant colors of the morning sunrise, or the amazing tenacity of a dandelion fighting to conquer its place in the grass.

When you begin to see and appreciate the richness around you, you will almost certainly find that you have a great deal more to be happy about than you once imagined.

Happiness is there for the taking.

Humor is to life what shock absorbers are to automobiles.

Albert Schweitzer

A cheerful heart is good medicine.

Proverbs 17:22 NIV

It isn't your position that makes you happy or unhappy, it's your disposition.

Godliness with contentment is great gain. For we brought nothing into this world, and it is certain we can carry nothing out.

1 Timothy 6:6-7 KJV

Have Your Best Year Ever . . .

In Fitness

The chief condition on which life, health, and vigor depend on, is action.
It is by action that an organism develops its faculties, increases its energy,
and attains the fulfillment of its destiny.

Colin Powell

Physical fitness is not only one of the most important keys to a healthy body, it is the basis of dynamic and creative intellectual activity.

John F. Kennedy

So many people are looking for the right solution for fitness and weight loss only to find frustration and fleeting improvement. It seems the only options are to try yet another, perhaps more drastic, measure or just give up altogether.

A more balanced approach includes easy-to-manage baby steps that lead to a change in thought, focus, and habits. A new lifestyle is adopted, in some ways without even realizing it, bringing with it weight loss and healthy living. The most important aspect of any plan is the ability to maintain your healthy lifestyle over a period of time.

January 1 is a date when most people seem to believe all things truly are possible—even the keeping of resolutions that were made the year before and were broken by February. No matter what day of the year it is, today is the first day of the rest of your life. Today is the day for a healthy change.

The dream of reaching and maintaining a healthy weight will never be realized unless you make a start. Develop a plan. Set a goal. And work the plan you've made. Patience and hard work are required to reach any worthy goal, but you can do it! If not now, when?

There is in this world no such force as a man determined to rise.
W. E. B. Du Bois

Success depends on backbone, not wishbone.

Start with the Numbers

Know where you stand before you start!

Before you commit yourself to stand firm until the weight comes off, pause to collect all the pertinent numbers related to your health—blood pressure, cholesterol count (both HDL and LDL), blood chemistry breakdown, and weight. Such a checkup will also serve to isolate any specific problems you may need to address with your physician.

This provides a clear benchmark in your mind and alerts you to any potential complications brought about by increased exercise and a change in diet. Check again in six months to see if you are making progress. Be faithful, and you should see numbers that truly make you feel good.

Be sure you put your feet in the right place. Then stand firm.
Abraham Lincoln

Points for Positive Progress:

- Realize you are changing your thoughts, focus and habits.
- Ask your doctor to help you set realistic goals.
- Ask for support from friends and family you trust.
- Pinpoint what stresses you out.
- Turn to exercise instead of food for comfort.
- Exercise for shorter periods several more times per day.
- Reward yourself for meeting your goals.
- Refuse to quit.

Perfect posture can make a plain person stunningly attractive. It can convey confidence and discipline. Yet in our fitness culture, we tend to focus on chiseling our abs, arms and buns, while posture maintenance gets pushed to the back burner. We sometimes even sacrifice good posture for a "good" workout, such as the "spinning slouch" or excessive neck tension caused by incorrect weight lifting. The good news is with a bit of knowledge and increased body awareness, great posture can be obtained.

What does great posture look like? Well, it's not rigid movement or a stiff back, it's not something to be turned on and off for a business meeting or family photo, nor is it only mom's job to promote proper posture; it's also the fitness trainer's job. People with good posture move effortlessly with poise, confidence, and fluidity. Their body awareness is stellar, making them true art in motion.[1]

1. Ellen Barrett, "Straighten Up! 4 Steps to Great Posture," *Fitness*, May–June 2004 http://www.findarticles.com/p/articles/mi_m0675/is_3_22/ai_n6057269

Good Posture

- Proper alignment allows the body to move like a well-oiled machine.
- Balance is knowing one's center and having the ability to readily locate it.
- Symmetry is balanced body proportions.
- Back health is composed of three parts—back strength, flexibility, and absence of restrictive tension. When back health is absent, back pain and poor posture exist.[2]

Pain has a message. The information it has about our life can be remarkably specific, but it usually falls into one of two categories: "We would be more alive if we did more of this," and, "Life would be more lovely if we did less of that." Once we get the pain's message, and follow its advice, the pain goes away.

Peter McWilliams

.. Ibid.

H_2O

Drink more water!

Medical researchers have discovered that water may be the single most important catalyst in losing weight and keeping it off. Water is a natural appetite suppressor and actually helps the body metabolize stored fat.

Studies show that a decrease in water intake causes fat deposits to increase, while an increase in water intake can actually reduce fat deposits. In addition, water helps the body flush away undesirable toxins and fatty globules from the bloodstream. It is a major aid to maintaining good digestion and elimination.

On the average, a person should drink eight glasses of water every day. An overweight person should add to that an extra glass of water for every twenty-five pounds of excess weight.

Open his eyes, shut off by the clouds from the thousand fountains so near him,
dying of thirst in his own desert.
Goethe

10 Reasons to Drink Water

1. Water is absolutely essential to the human body's survival. A person can live for about a month without food, but only about a week without water.
2. Water helps to maintain healthy body weight by increasing metabolism and regulating appetite.
3. Water leads to increased energy levels. The most common cause of daytime fatigue is actually mild dehydration.
4. Drinking adequate amounts of water can decrease the risk of certain types of cancers, including colon cancer, bladder cancer, and breast cancer.
5. For a majority of sufferers, drinking water can significantly reduce joint and/or back pain.
6. Water leads to overall greater health by flushing out wastes and bacteria that can cause disease.
7. Water can prevent and alleviate headaches.
8. Water naturally moisturizes skin and ensures proper cellular formation underneath layers of skin to give it a healthy, glowing appearance.
9. Water aids in the digestion process and prevents constipation.
10. Water is the primary mode of transportation for all nutrients in the body and is essential for proper circulation.[3]

---

3. "10 Reasons to Drink Water" Copyright © 2004 All About Water.org. All rights reserved. http://www.allaboutwater.org/drink-water.html

Nutrients

For decades people have believed that eating a balanced diet provided all the nutrients they needed. It's simply not true

—Michael Janson, M.D. (*Health and Nutrition Breakthroughs,* March 1998).

Food cravings can be a signal that key nutrients are missing from your diet or that they are not being supplied in adequate amounts. Unfortunately, we often seek to satisfy cravings with foods that are high in calories, sugars, and fat. What many people don't know is that cravings for wrong foods—such as chocolate and sugary foods—can actually be eliminated over time by eating foods higher in protein.

To make certain that you receive all of the micro-nutrients your body needs in adequate quantities, consider adding vitamins, minerals, and protein supplements to your weight-loss plan. Work with a nutritionist to determine the best options or simply ask your physician or pharmacist. It's so important to feed your cells all the nutrients they need.

Myth: High-protein/low-carbohydrate diets are a healthy way to lose weight.

Fact: The long-term health effects of a high-protein/low-carbohydrate diet are unknown. But getting most of your daily calories from high-protein foods like meat, eggs, and cheese is not a balanced eating plan. You may be eating too much fat and cholesterol, which may raise heart disease risk. You may be eating too few fruits, vegetables, and whole grains, which may lead to constipation due to lack of dietary fiber. Following a high-protein/low-carbohydrate diet may also make you feel nauseous, tired, and weak.

Tip: High-protein/low-carbohydrate diets are often low in calories because food choices are strictly limited, so they may cause short-term weight loss. But a reduced-calorie eating plan that includes recommended amounts of carbohydrate, protein, and fat will also allow you to lose weight.[4]

---

[4]. Weight Control Information Network, "Weight Loss and Nutrition Myths" NIH Publication No. 04-4561 March 2004 Posted: April 2004 http://win.niddk.nih.gov/publications/myths.htm

Set Training Goals

A woman with muscular dystrophy spent years saying, "I can't" to things she wanted to do. One day she decided to set a goal to run the New York City marathon. Much to the surprise of many, she finished the race and accomplished her goal! It was painful for her to prepare for the race and painful to run it, but she later told the world that every step was worth the pain.

To keep yourself motivated in an exercise program, set a training goal—perhaps to walk a mile in eight minutes, row across a local lake, hike a certain trail, or swim a half mile. Set incremental goals for achieving your final training goal. Then focus and begin "the race."

Every hour of activity is an hour of calorie expenditure.

Obstacles are those frightful things you see when you take your eyes off your goal.

Henry Ford

Setting a goal is not the main thing. It is deciding how you will go about achieving it and staying with that plan.

Tom Landry

Pain is temporary. It may last a minute, or an hour, or a day, or a year, but eventually it will subside and something else will take its place. If I quit, however, it lasts forever.

Lance Armstrong

I do not run like a man running aimlessly; I do not fight like a man beating the air.

1 Corinthians 9:26 NIV

Have Your Best Year Ever . . .

In Business

Real integrity is doing the right thing,

knowing that nobody's going to know whether you did it or not.

Oprah Winfrey

Ambition, fueled by compassion, wisdom, and integrity is a powerful force for good that will turn the wheels of industry and open the doors of opportunity for you and countless others.

Zig Ziglar

Always try to maintain complete tolerance and always make an effort to give people more than they expect.

Scott Hamilton

You probably know someone who overflows with excitement in their work, their hobby, or simply their life. We find their infectious enthusiasm hard to resist. If you're around them for long, the next thing you know, you get caught up in their excitement.

There are others who could make creation itself seem like just another string of scientific equations. For all their vast learning and impressive vocabulary, they've sacrificed the sense of wonder they were born with. The difference between the two is passion. Passion fuels the dream and drives the desire to get to your dream and reach your destiny. Passion challenges you to reach out and take what you imagined.

Pursue your passion in life. Share it with others. Become known as a person of infectious enthusiasm. What's in your heart? What have you always wanted to do? Find success by reaching for that which is already within you.

Nothing great in the world has been accomplished without passion.
Georg Wilheim Freidrich Hegel

Be still when you have nothing to say; when genuine passion moves you, say what you've got to say, and say it hot.
D. H. Lawrence

The most untutored person with passion is more persuasive than the most eloquent without.
Francois de la Rochefoucauld

I know your eagerness to help. . . your enthusiasm has stirred most of them to action.
2 Corinthians 9:2 NIV

I make progress by having people around me who are smarter than I am—and listening to them.

Harry J. Kaiser

The difference between ordinary and extraordinary is that little "extra."

Most of the things worth doing in the world had been declared impossible before they were done.

Conrad Hilton

A man is not finished when he is defeated. He is finished when he quits.

Fight the good fight of faith.

1 Timothy 6:12 KJV

People of Action

What makes a person a great success? Some believe great achievers are born, and others are sure they are made. Harry Truman once said, "Men make history and not the other way around. In periods where there is no leadership, society stands still. Progress occurs when courageous, skilled leaders seize the opportunity to change things for the better."

Successful people are those with integrity, principle, and self-control, more interested in serving others than themselves. They are people of action. They motivate others, yet they are never afraid to take responsibility. They encourage others to fulfill their dreams.

A great man is always willing to serve others.

Success is:

- Measured by the challenges you face and overcome.
- Hard work.
- Steady perseverance.
- Consistent common sense.
- Sincere self-confidence.
- Knowing how to get along with people.
- Aiming high.
- Trying over and over and over again.
- A decision to succeed.

Success is not:

- Spontaneous.
- Measured by wealth, influence, or fame.
- Almost, but not quite.
- Just doing something that is "good enough."
- Putting yourself on top at the expense of others.
- A fleeting moment of trial and error.
- Knowledge alone.
- Waiting for your ship to come in.
- A shortcut.
- About money.
- Repeating the same mistakes.

Strength in Endurance

The film *Amazon*, made for the huge IMAX screen, shows the incredible resiliency of the rainforests of the Amazon River basin. The trees and wildlife flourish in conditions that look very difficult to the casual observer. During the rainy season, forty-seven feet of water can cover the basin floor! But this flooding serves a purpose, and the inhabitants of the Amazon make the most of it.

The floodwaters benefit the native people by providing a habitat for specific fish. Only during this time of high waters can the natives find an abundance of this fish. The root systems of the trees grow more readily when deeply submersed, and in turn they feed and protect the tree dwellers that are vital to the ecosystem. "Going with the flow" seems to be the motto of the Amazon.

Perhaps you've felt the floodwaters rise around you. The stresses of work can pour down. You might feel like you could drown. But if you take hold of the rock of God's grace, you can begin to see the rainy season in your life as a time of growth. The rushing waters of difficulty can bring an abundance of strength your way.

Perhaps the strange and wonderful cycles of the Amazon hold a lesson for us in seeing our dreams realized. As you go with the flow, rather than resisting the river of change, you might find more than just personal growth at the end of your journey. Endurance could bring your dream closer to reality.

When written in Chinese, the word "crisis" is composed of two characters—one represents danger, and the other represents opportunity.

John F. Kennedy

Sometimes we stare so long at a door that is closing that we see too late the one that is open.

Alexander Graham Bell

Small opportunities are often the beginning of great enterprises.

Demothenes

Opportunity is missed by most people because it is dressed in overalls and looks like work.

Thomas Edison

Create Opportunity

As many people learned in recent years, job security is a thing of the past. Even where you can still find company loyalty, you can't always count on company longevity. Many who expected to retire after a lifetime with the same company found themselves downsized into a whole new career choice, but others found themselves in the unemployment lines.

The difference in these two groups is opportunity. Some, to be sure, had it handed to them, but many who found new careers created their own opportunity. Many of those who seemed to have no way out may have failed to recognize an opportunity.

The Bible says all things work together for the good of those who love him (Romans 8:28 NIV). We must apply that to misfortune as well as success. Events that first seem bleak can steer us in an exciting new direction if we keep our eyes, ears, and mind open and alert for opportunities that cross our path.

Have Your Best Year Ever . . .

In Your Heart and Soul

To know what you prefer instead of humbly saying Amen to what the world tells you, you ought to prefer, is to have kept your soul alive.

Robert Louis Stevenson

God is our true friend, who always gives us the counsel and comfort we need. Our danger lies in resisting him; so it is essential that we acquire the habit of hearkening to his voice, or keeping silence within, and listening so as to lose nothing of what he says to us. We know well enough how to keep outward silence, and to hush our spoken words, but we know little of interior silence. It consists in hushing our idle, restless, wandering imagination, in quieting the promptings of our worldly minds, and in suppressing the crowd of unprofitable thoughts which excite and disturb the soul.

François Fénelon

Today more than ever before people are looking for answers to the questions: Who am I? Why am I here? and What's God got to do with it? The lowly carpenter's son from Nazareth lived and died almost two thousand years ago. His life, which only lasted thirty-three years, was not remarkable on any grand scale. In fact, he lived in relative obscurity until three years before his death. When he did move out of the shadows and speak openly, the words of this unpretentious folk leader were recorded by only a few of his disciples.

Nevertheless, the simple words of Jesus Christ have endured throughout the centuries, inspiring, motivating, and enriching the lives of millions of people. Jesus had much to say about his mission and his relationship with God.

In his examples we find extraordinary wisdom, the power to change long-standing perceptions, rethink priorities, and live significant and fulfilled lives. We can find the answers to the questions everyone is asking through the words of Jesus and our own relationship with God.

God is a spirit: and they that worship him must worship him in spirit and in truth.
Jesus (John 4:24 KJV)

God so loved the world that he gave his one and only Son, that whoever believes in him shall not perish but have eternal life.
Jesus (John 3:16 NIV)

Your Father knows exactly what you need even before you ask him!
Jesus (Matthew 6:8 NLT)

Trust God

Life can be a frightening, difficult, and lonely experience. Isn't it good to know there is someone who watches over us and never leaves us in the best and the worst of it all? You can simplify your life today by placing your cares in the hollow of God's hand.

The Bible quotes the Psalmist who said, "I will lift my eyes unto the hills, from whence cometh my help. My help cometh from the Lord, which made heaven and earth" (Psalm 121:1-2 KJV). These words were penned by a man who knew the peace and comfort of resting in the care of someone greater than himself.

That same peace and comfort is available to anyone who will ask for it. Why worry when you can talk to God?

Blessed are all they that put their trust in him.
Psalm 2:12 KJV

The measure of a man's character is not what he gets from his ancestors, but what he leaves his descendants.

The measure of a man is not how great his faith is but how great his love is.

When God measures a man, he puts the tape around the heart instead of the head.

The LORD seeth not as man seeth; for man looketh on the outward appearance, but the LORD looketh on the heart.

1 Samuel 16:7 KJV

More

If someone were to ask why Jesus came to the earth, you'd answer: "He came to save us from eternal punishment." You'd be right, but there's more: He also came to give us life in the here-and-now, an abundant life.

Many of us feel more like we're hanging by a thread. Abundant life? What's that? All we see is work, bills, family problems, and worse—boredom. Maybe Sunday mornings feel better if we're in church, and occasionally we've seen God work in our lives; but the abundant life seems to have passed us by on a daily basis.

Your heart yearns for more, but you don't know what to do about it? Give yourself completely to God. Then follow your heart. You have permission to do that. The Bible says that God will give you the desires of your heart when your heart is turned toward him.

God gave you a dream for an abundant life that resides within you!

I came that they may have life, and have it abundantly.
Jesus (John 10:10 NASB)

By whatever basis human desires are classified, the promise of an abundant life covers virtually all. To the spiritual it suggests escape from futility; to the sensuous it calls up visions of luxury; to the defeated it is a dream of success. To the idle it pledges ease; to the weary, rest; to the frightened it means safety; to the anxious, security; and to the improvident it conjures inexhaustible resources. Persuade a man that you can give him the thing he most desires and you will be his hero; offer him justification for his failures and he will be your disciple; assure him a boundless supply of "loaves and fishes" and he will seek to make you king.

Samuel Parkes Cadman

God can heal a broken heart, but he has to have all the pieces.

In order to receive the direction from God, you must be able to receive the correction from God.

I Believe I Could Touch Heaven if I:

- Was more thankful for what I have.
- Talked to God more like a friend.
- Listened more closely to what my heart says.
- Was more transparent with those God puts in my life.
- Read my Bible more with a desire for understanding.
- Was willing to give.
- Esteemed others more highly than myself.
- Offered praise to God just because I can.

Praise is the voice of faith. It sings the story of a victorious battle in the midst of difficulty and circumstance long before the answer comes—before the battle is won.

Let your actions and the words of your mouth give praise to God.

Praise to the Lord, the Almighty, who rules all creation! O my soul, worship the source of thy health and salvation! All yet who hear, now to God's temple draw near; join me in glad adoration!
Joachim Neander, "Praise to the Lord, the Almighty"

I will praise You, O LORD, with my whole heart; I will tell of all Your marvelous works.
Psalm 9:1 NKJV

What a Journey?

The perfect shell sat half buried in a small pile of rocks, its spiral silhouette unbroken by the pounding surf. Jeremy picked it up and dusted off the sticky grains of sand. Although he walked this beach every morning, a shell like this was a rare find. The shore was littered with bits of shell, coral, and smoothly sanded glass, but the rocks and the fierceness of the sea deposited most of its treasures here in pieces. What a journey this shell must have had, Jeremy thought. He couldn't help but think of his own rocky journey over the past few years. He could finally look back on it and see how God had brought him through, unbroken.

Jeremy put the shell in his pocket, a reminder to see God's faithfulness during difficult times.

When outward strength is broken, faith rests on the promises.
Robert Cecil

Your path led through the sea, your way through the mighty waters, though your footprints were not seen.
Psalm 77:19 NIV

This poor man cried out, and the LORD heard him, and saved him out of all his troubles.
Psalm 34:6 NKJV

What do you long for? The small group leader had posed this same question twelve weeks earlier. Back then Terry had known exactly what to say. "I long for someone special to love, a chance to play my music, and enough money to live independently." Others had offered similar responses. But now, after all they'd studied and explored together, the answer wasn't so simple.

"I'm not quite sure what I long for," Terry began. "Perhaps it's a chance to know God more intimately." Others nodded, then added their insights. One thing was certain—he knew what longing was now. Those things he'd mentioned twelve weeks ago? Sure, he still dreamed of them, but his longing was something deeper.

Your deepest longings are placed within you by God and can't be filled with anything other than his presence.

God is never found accidentally.
A. W. Tozer

In quiet moments with the Father or times of spiritual reflection, it may be easy to feel his presence. Perhaps it's a different matter when you're driving to work, paying the bills, or heading to the dentist. If only you could feel connected to God in the everyday tasks of life.

God cares about every step you take, and he longs to be your permanent companion no matter where you go. God is in your everyday life. He stands ready for you to tell him everything and offer you the peace of mind you want. As you reach out to him and open your heart, you will encounter the depths of his love and his commitment to walk with you moment by moment.

The Lord is near.
Philippians 4:5 NIV

References

Additional copies of this
and other Honor products are available
wherever good books are sold.

If you have enjoyed this book,
or if it has had an impact on your life,
we would like to hear from you.

Please contact us at:

Honor Books
Cook Communications Ministries, Dept. 201
4050 Lee Vance View
Colorado Springs, CO 80918
Or visit our Web site: www.cookministries.com